BROUGHAM AND BROUGH CASTLES

CUMBRIA

Henry Summerson

The castles at Brougham and Brough, built in medieval times, were both held by the same two families for almost the whole of their history, first by the Vieuxponts and then, for over four centuries, by the Cliffords. One of the most important visitors to Brougham was Edward I, who spent a night in the castle in 1300. The castle later played host to James I and his court in 1617. Both castles fell into ruins in the eighteenth century, and Brougham's decaying shell inspired Wordsworth in his great poem 'The Prelude'.

This guidebook is divided into two sections, the first on Brougham and the second on Brough. It also includes a fascinating portrait of Lady Anne, the most famous of the Cliffords.

❖ CONTENTS ❖

- 3 INTRODUCTION
- 4 BROUGHAM CASTLE: HISTORY
  - 4 THE CASTLE IN THE VALLEY
  - 5 THE CASTLE IN ITS HEYDAY
  - 6 NEGLECT AND DECAY
  - 6 BROUGHAM'S RENAISSANCE
  - 7 LATER HISTORY
- 9 BROUGHAM CASTLE: TOUR
  - 9 THE GATEHOUSE
  - 11 THE COURTYARD
  - 12 THE TOWER OF LEAGUE
  - 13 LODGINGS FOR THE GARRISON
  - 13 THE CHAPEL
  - 14 THE COVERED PASSAGE
  - 14 THE INNER COURTYARD AND WELL
  - 14 THE KITCHEN AND HALL
  - 15 THE GREAT CHAMBER
  - 15 THE KEEP
  - 16 The First Floor
  - 17 The Second Floor
  - 18 The Third Floor
- 21 LADY ANNE CLIFFORD
- 26 BIRD'S-EYE VIEWS OF BROUGHAM AND BROUGH
- 28 BROUGH CASTLE: HISTORY
  - 28 THE CASTLE ON THE RIDGE
  - 30 BROUGH UNDER THE CLIFFORDS
  - 31 BROUGH'S RENAISSANCE
  - 32 LATER HISTORY
- 33 BROUGH CASTLE: TOUR
  - 33 THE GATEHOUSE
  - 34 THE COURTYARD
  - 34 THE STABLES
  - 34 THE KEEP
  - 36 THE BREWHOUSE, BAKEHOUSE AND KITCHEN
  - 37 THE HALL RANGE
    - 37 The Laundress's Room
    - 37 The Hall
    - 38 The Great Chamber
  - 38 THE CHURCH OF ST MICHAEL
- 39 BIBLIOGRAPHY
- 40 PLANS

Published by English Heritage, 1 Waterhouse Square, 138–142 Holborn, London EC1N 2ST
© English Heritage 1999 First published by English Heritage 1999
Reprinted 2004, 2006, 2012
Revised reprint 2010, 2014
Photographs by English Heritage Photographic Unit and copyright of English Heritage, unless otherwise stated.

We are grateful to the Dean and Chapter of Carlisle Cathedral for permission to reproduce the Machell drawings on pages 35 and 36; to Colin Edwards for permission to use the photographs of gargoyles on pages 15 and 18; and to Skipton Castle for permission to use the portraits on pages 7 and 22. (Skipton Castle in North Yorkshire is open all year round, except Christmas Day.)

Edited by Susannah Lawson
Designed by Pauline Hull. Plans by Hardlines
Printed in England by Park Communications Ltd
C25 07/14 04757 ISBN 978-1-85074-729-1

INTRODUCTION

❖

The settings of the castles of Brougham and Brough could hardly be more different. Brougham stands in a river valley, in a peaceful landscape of fields and woods; Brough, in contrast, occupies a bleak and exposed position, open to the gales that blow round the surrounding Pennines. Yet differences of geography apart, the two castles have a good deal in common, not least their names. Both contain the Old English word 'burh', meaning a fortified place, and in both cases the fortifications in question were older than the castles, referring to the Roman forts which once occupied the sites.

The strategic positions which encouraged the Romans to build at Brougham and Brough also led to the construction of medieval castles there. Brough is the elder of the two, but from the time Brougham was built, early in the thirteenth century, both were held by the same two families for almost the whole of their history, first by the Vieuxponts and then, for over four centuries, by the Cliffords. For both families these two castles were as much centres of their regional power as they were strongholds designed to resist their enemies, whether these were Scots or rival members of the English nobility. In the seventeenth century, they both enjoyed a last lease of life, thanks to the life and works of the most famous of all the Cliffords, the redoubtable Lady Anne, who died at Brougham in 1676. Both castles subsequently lost nearly all their roofs, floors and furnishings, which were sold by Lady Anne's grandson, the sixth earl of Thanet, at almost exactly the same time – Brougham in 1714 and Brough a year later. As a result both fell steadily into ruin, before coming into the care of the Ministry of Works, the precursor of English Heritage, Brough in 1919 and Brougham in 1928.

SKYSCAN BALLOON PHOTOGRAPHY

Aerial views of Brougham (above) and Brough Castles (below), showing the outlines of the Roman forts Brocavum and Verteris

BROUGHAM CASTLE HISTORY

THE CASTLE IN THE VALLEY

In about 1214, Robert de Vieuxpont, one of King John's most important agents in the north of England, acquired the site on which Brougham Castle was later built, in order to defend his lands against his royal master's northern enemies and their Scottish allies. It was a good site for a castle. Protected on its north and west sides by the rivers Eamont and Lowther, it commands the crossing of the Eamont just to the east, and controls nearby roads running north to south and east to west. The Romans had built here for the same reason, and the ruins of the fort of *Brocavum* provided stone for building as well as earthworks which could be adapted for medieval purposes.

Vieuxpont's castle consisted of a stone keep and service buildings, surrounded by a timber palisade, which was replaced by a stone curtain wall in around 1300. By then the castle was in the hands of Robert Clifford, whose father Roger had become lord of Brougham when he married Robert de Vieuxpont's great-granddaughter in 1268 (refer to the family tree on the inside front cover). Robert Clifford was an

Brougham Castle, seen in all its strength from across the River Eamont

important figure in the Scottish wars which started in 1296. The works which he carried out at Brougham – the gatehouse complex, the top storey of the keep, the Tower of League at the south-west corner of the castle bailey, and the stone curtain walls – both proclaimed his standing and strengthened the defences against attack by the Scots.

The Castle in its Heyday

The Anglo-Scottish wars which began under Edward I lasted for centuries. Further works became necessary under Robert's grandson, Roger Clifford, in the 1380s. He was responsible for a number of buildings along the south curtain wall, including a new hall which had over its door the stone carved 'Thys Made Roger', now to be seen over the outer gatehouse. But these could not prevent a damaging Scottish raid in 1388, when the castle was captured and sacked. It is not known to have been back in use until 1421, when a man was accused of forging coins inside its walls!

Brougham was important in the Wars of the Roses, as Lancastrian Cliffords and Yorkist Nevilles competed for dominance in north-west England. It occupied a strategic position, and for that reason was granted to the Nevilles by Edward IV

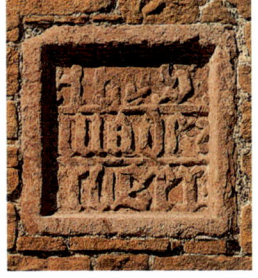

Stone carved 'Thys made Roger', originally put up in the 1380s by Roger, fifth Lord Clifford, over the door to his new hall, but set in the outer gatehouse in the mid-nineteenth century

Brougham Castle in the early thirteenth century, when the keep was surrounded by a timber palisade. Reconstruction drawing by Peter Dunn

Above: Portrait of James I, after John de Critz (detail). He was entertained in Brougham Castle at enormous expense in 1617

Right: George Clifford, third earl of Cumberland, portrayed by Nicholas Hilliard in his armour as Queen Elizabeth's champion (detail). He was born at Brougham Castle in 1558

after John Clifford was killed fighting for Henry VI in 1461. But John's son Henry (sometimes called 'the shepherd lord' in the ill-founded belief that he was brought up in rustic obscurity to keep him out of harm's way after his father's death), recovered Brougham and the rest of his family's estates from Henry VII, and under the Tudors he and his family prospered. Henry's son, another Henry Clifford (c.1493–1542), was made earl of Cumberland in 1525, and his son, yet another Henry (1517–70), spent much time at Brougham, where his son and heir, George, the third earl, was born in 1558.

Neglect and Decay

In George's time, however, the castle was increasingly neglected, as its lord spent more and more time at court, where he acted as Queen Elizabeth I's champion. An inventory of 1595, which covers the castle in detail, reveals a sorry state of affairs, with room after room either sparsely fitted out with old and decayed furniture, or piled with ancient armour, decayed pots and pans, and junk. But when George died in 1605, the castle came back to life again for a while, as the dower-house of his widow, Countess Margaret. In 1617, the year after her death, James I and his court were received at Brougham, spending two nights in the castle. The expense to George's brother Francis, the fourth earl, was vast. He had to lay on exotic food like peachicks and quails, and also an elaborate masque, in which singers, dancers and musicians united to entertain and praise the king.

Brougham's Renaissance

The castle was then neglected again, and though it was manned by the Royalists, it played little part in the Civil Wars of the 1640s. But it enjoyed an Indian summer after 1650 thanks to George's daughter, Lady Anne Clifford, who restored the fabric of the castle, added a new bakehouse and brewhouse, and laid out a substantial garden for fruit and vegetables on the south side of the castle. She paid repeated and extended visits to Brougham, with a large household, and finally died in the castle on 22 March 1676. The castle was maintained for a while after her death, and a man was paid to clean the roofs and rooms up to the beginning of 1714. But by then the earl of Thanet had decided that he did not need all his ancestral castles, and that one at Appleby was enough. That year he sold all the castle's furnishings and fittings, apart from those of the Tower of League, for £570. Nine years later, in 1723, the Tower of League was similarly disposed of, fetching a further £40 5s.

LATER HISTORY

Reduced to an empty and roofless shell, the castle quickly fell into ruin. Its appearance of picturesque decay was increasingly admired by visitors and passers-by. In the late 1840s the last earl of Thanet carried out substantial works to preserve what was left of its fabric. But his successors, the Lords Hothfield, soon found the burden of maintenance too heavy.

Above: Portrait of Thomas Tufton, sixth earl of Thanet, (detail) who stripped Brougham to the stonework in the early eighteenth century

Below: Brougham Castle, in an engraving of 1739, by the Buck Brothers. Only fifteen years after it had gone out of use, the castle was fast falling into ruin

By 1859 cattle were being kept in the gatehouse, and visitors often complained that parts of the castle were ruinous or inaccessible, or both. Finally, in 1928 the castle was put into the guardianship of the Ministry of Works, which proceeded to remove as much as possible of the masonry inserted so expensively in the 1840s. Brougham Castle appears today essentially as the Ministry of Works left it in the 1930s.

❖ WORDSWORTH & BROUGHAM ❖

William Wordsworth (1770–1850) was born at Cockermouth and grew up in the Lake District. His upbringing there provided lasting inspiration towards his development as a poet. Changes in taste also led to tourists coming to the Lakes and the regions around in increasing numbers in the late eighteenth century, drawn by the beauties of a landscape which had previously been dismissed as intolerably bleak and monotonous. Under the influence of the increasingly influential Romantic movement, they admired the decaying ruins of castles like Brougham as well. But no travel-writer could match the eloquence with which Wordsworth, in his great poem 'The Prelude', described how he and his sister Dorothy would in their teens clamber among the ruins of Brougham Castle:

Portrait of William Wordsworth, in 1798, when he was in his late twenties, by Robert Haycock

*…That river and those mouldering towers
Have seen us side by side, when, having clomb
The darksome windings of a broken stair,
And crept along a ridge of fractured wall,
Not without trembling, we in safety looked
Forth, through some Gothic window's open space,
And gathered with one mind a rich reward
From the far-stretching landscape…*

BROUGHAM CASTLE TOUR

Walk down the path from the shop and exhibition to the gatehouse.

Brougham Castle is a complex structure – one that has been built, rebuilt, patched up and added to over several centuries. It may help to refer to the phased plan on p.40 as you go round.

THE GATEHOUSE

The gatehouse looks like a single, unified structure, but it is in fact made up of three elements – an outer and inner gatehouse with a courtyard between them. The outer gatehouse was built after the inner one. Peacetime visitors would have been observed from the guardroom in the north wall (on your right as you come through the gatehouse passage). The gatekeeper must also have been a gaoler, as there is a dungeon under the floor. The castle was probably intended to have only one gatehouse at first; what is now the inner gatehouse would certainly have been self-sufficient, with its own portcullis and gates. But around 1300, when Robert Clifford was lord of Brougham, something stronger was needed. Two gatehouses a few yards apart, with a courtyard between them, met this need.

Walk through the outer gatehouse into the inner courtyard.

The approach to the gatehouse: a solid late thirteenth-century structure with two storeys above the gateway

The inner gatehouse seen from inside the courtyard

Each gatehouse had two storeys above its gate-passage, while the courtyard had a block of lodgings on the side facing the river. So if enemies broke through the defences of the first gatehouse, before they could tackle those of the second, they would come under attack in this inner courtyard from missiles flung down from the upper floors of both gatehouses, from the keep and from the block facing it. A more effective killing ground is hard to imagine.

Cross the inner courtyard and stop when you reach the inner gatehouse passage.

The inner gatehouse also contains an observation point, this time for the postern gate which was cut into the western of the two outside buttresses, providing a way in and out of the castle when the main gate was closed.

To see this, go up the stairs on the right and follow the passage round.

This chamber allowed a watchman to keep an eye on the postern gate opposite, and on those who used it, as they came down the stairs from the floor above, where the portcullis machinery was operated.

Turn round and leave this chamber, and cross the gatehouse passage into another small room.

The window in this chamber is placed so as to enable its occupant to look out over the courtyard, and over those who entered the castle.

Return to the gatehouse passage and carry on into the courtyard.

There might have been a further purpose behind the construction of the gatehouse complex. It was important for medieval noblemen to display their power and wealth, and there was a theatrical side to their lifestyles. The Brougham gatehouses, with the castle's main courtyard beyond, had something of the character of a stage-set, and we can imagine exciting processions as the lord of Brougham and his followers, flags on spears, plumes on helmets, cloaks flying out behind, swept in through the gates and round towards the keep. One of the most important visitors to Brougham was Edward I, who spent the night of 22 July 1300 at the castle. With the Scottish war bringing Edward regularly to the borders, Robert Clifford could reasonably have expected further visits (though none are in fact recorded). When the king stayed in another man's house, it became his for as long as he remained in it. Yet another motive for Robert Clifford's improving and adding to his castle at Brougham might well have been the prospect of having to provide suitable accommodation for the king and his court.

The Courtyard

The medieval visitor would usually have continued round to the left, to the keep, which was the heart of the castle.

But, for the purposes of the tour, continue on the paved footpath along the west curtain wall, and go in an anti-clockwise direction round the castle, leaving the keep till last.

The courtyard to your left was probably always cobbled (in wet weather a grass surface would quickly have been trampled into a quagmire by men and horses) though what you see now may well owe something of its regularity to Lady Anne Clifford. The west wall of the castle (on your right) was lined with buildings which have now entirely vanished. They would have included the stables and

The arrival of Edward I at Brougham on 22 July 1300. Reconstruction drawing by Peter Dunn

the bakehouse and brewhouse recorded in the 1595 inventory. The last two buildings were replaced by Lady Anne Clifford in 1662, in order to make the courtyard 'larger and hansomer than it was before'. All would have been at ground level, but with storage rooms above. As you approach the south-west corner, you will come to another postern gate, opening onto the causeway which crosses the moat outside. However, the postern gate is a good deal older than the causeway, which was probably constructed for Lady Anne Clifford. Back inside the castle, you can see near the postern gate one of the few additions to the castle identifiable as having been made by Lady Anne – the bread oven whose outline can be seen on the right a few yards from the foot of the corner tower.

Walk down the steps and go through the doorway into the basement of the tower.

The Tower of League

This great tower was built by Robert Clifford in about 1300, and it had an important defensive role, not just against attackers outside the walls, but also against any enemies who broke in through the gatehouses and hoped to storm the keep. It was referred to in 1723 as the 'Tower of Liege', which might have been its original name, meaning the tower of lordship, in reference to its commanding position at the south end of the castle. It was also used as a residence. Each of its four floors constituted a single chamber, each with a latrine and fireplace, suggesting that it was intended for important and favoured guests.

Go back up the steps and out of the tower and turn right along the path round the courtyard.

On your right is a well, which would have provided drinking water and would also have been useful for cleaning the courtyard and the lodgings (think of the mess made by large numbers of horses!)

Go through the doorway on the right, just past the well.

The Tower of League, built by Robert Clifford in about 1300

Lodgings for the Garrison

These are the castle's communal rooms, where the garrison gathered to eat, sleep or pray, often under the eye or in the company of the lord. This first room most probably formed part of a block of lodgings, three floors high at first, and later reduced to two. Its date is uncertain; it could have been built by Roger Clifford in response to the Scottish threat of the 1380s, or it might have been another addition made by his grandfather. Either way, it provides clear evidence for the castle's military function, and its need, in times of crisis at any rate, to give shelter to a substantial number of fighting men. Provision was made for their most basic needs. Looking up at the east wall of the lodgings at first-floor level, there is a window looking into the chapel, with a door to the left of it, also giving access to the chapel, and an entrance to a latrine on the right. Above these the outline of a pitched roof shows the level of the building after it was reduced in height, presumably in the days when a large garrison was no longer needed.

Carry on through the far doorway.

The Chapel

This room was once the chapel, also built by Roger Clifford. Like the lodgings, it was probably intended for

The lodgings for the garrison, where the soldiers slept

the use of the larger garrison of the 1380s. In 1385, Roger Clifford had thirty men-at-arms (cavalrymen) and sixty archers at Brougham, as well as the usual garrison. The latter was probably small, but in the late fourteenth century there could well have been a hundred fighting men in the castle, all needing somewhere to eat and sleep, to keep their equipment and horses, and to worship; the castle must have been packed with people. The chapel was a building of fine quality. It was on the first floor, above a basement, so you will have to look up to admire its graceful three-arched *sedilia* (seats for clergy), and the little *piscina* (the basin in which the sacred vessels were washed) immediately to the left of them, as well as the two deeply-set windows higher up to the right.

Before you move on, turn left in the direction of the keep.

The three-arched sedilia *in the fourteenth-century chapel; high-class work carried out for Roger Clifford*

The Covered Passage

You will see the outline on the ground of a long structure running to the south-east corner of the keep. Two or three storeys high, it once provided a covered passage from the upper floors of the keep to the chapel. Although Roger Clifford inherited a private oratory on the top floor of the keep, he knew that the conventions of lordship required him to take his place among his men when they gathered to worship. We can imagine him or his heirs making their way along this corridor from the keep into the chapel, to join the men of the garrison as they prayed for victory or safety.

Walk through the doorway at the far end of the chapel.

The remains of the hall and kitchen; they, too, were commissioned by Roger Clifford

The Inner Courtyard and Well

This small courtyard contains one of the castle's wells. Beyond it stood the kitchen, built, as was usually the case, as close as possible to the water supply, which was essential both for cooking and cleaning. A causeway across the Roman fort ends against the castle wall outside this courtyard, raising the possibility that, perhaps before the stone curtain wall was built, this was the castle's original entrance.

Walk through the doorway on the far side of the courtyard.

The Kitchen and Hall

The room in which you are standing was once the basement of the kitchen. Next to it was the castle's second hall, built in the time of Roger Clifford.

In order to get a better view of the hall, go back into the courtyard, past the well and through the passage. Turn right just at the end of the covered passageway.

The stone carved 'Thys Made Roger', now above the gatehouse, was originally set over the entrance to the hall, which was reached by a flight of stone stairs set within a porch. It was probably the outbreak of Anglo-Scottish hostilities in 1384 which made Roger decide that a new hall, like a new chapel, was needed, to accommodate a greatly enlarged garrison. A medieval nobleman needed to show himself to, and mix with, his retainers and followers if he was to ensure their loyalty, and one way he did this was by eating with them. Hence the importance of the hall in a castle. Roger Clifford's new hall was clearly another building of quality, as the handsome windows in the outer wall make clear. They are surprisingly large for a defensive building, although they would doubtless have been covered by heavy wooden shutters when the need arose. The hall would have been warmed by at least one fireplace in its east wall, and it is also possible that there was a central hearth. Roger would have eaten on a dais, or platform, raising him slightly above the level of his social inferiors at the north end of the hall. He would have faced the door into the kitchen, and food would have been brought directly to his table, to be carved and distributed.

THE GREAT CHAMBER

After a meal, Roger Clifford and his family would have retired through a door behind them into the great chamber. This room used to be the hall, but it was later converted into the great chamber, a private room for the lord. The shape of the great chamber is now preserved only by the grass-covered open space at the north end of the hall. In the thirteenth century (probably when it was built) it formed part of a three-storey structure, with a basement under it, while the top floor might have contained the nursery recorded in the 1595 inventory.

Walk through the remains of the great chamber and into the basement of the keep.

THE KEEP

The keep is the earliest part of the castle still standing. The bottom three storeys are the oldest, and they have often been dated to around

A decorative corbel on the outside of the keep

The outline of the great chamber, seen from the top of the keep. The lord and his family would have retired here after a meal

The keep, seen over the south curtain wall. Even in ruins it dominates the rest of the castle

The remains of the original stairs to the keep

1175, on the basis of their stylistic similarity to other castles of that time. However, since the documentary evidence suggests that the keep cannot have been begun before the second decade of the thirteenth century, one can only suppose that Robert de Vieuxpont either had old-fashioned tastes when it came to building a castle, or that he employed an elderly or old-fashioned mason. The fact that the entrance was on the east side meant that anyone who had fought his way through the gatehouses would still have had to go right round the keep in order to approach its entrance. In the meantime, they would have been exposed to attack from above, and also (after about 1300) from the Tower of League in the south-west corner of the courtyard, which was easily within bowshot. Even then, access was blocked, for the doorway was on the first floor, and it was covered by a substantial forebuilding, which doubtless had a strong door of its own.

The basement in which you are standing was originally used as a store. Nineteenth-century visitors were impressed by its elegant vault, supported by a central octagonal column, which has regrettably now vanished. They imagined, inaccurately, that it was once a prison or torture chamber, instead of just a depot for sacks of flour and barrels of beer. The floors of the keep were connected by a staircase in its north-east corner (on your right as you come in to the basement). You can still climb the stairs to the upper storeys, though the disappearance of the floors means that we can only imagine how the rooms – one per storey – were used.

Stop on the stairs when you reach the first floor.

The First Floor

Notice the remains of column capitals and arcading along the west wall and in the south-east corner. This was probably a reception room, and its simple but graceful decoration – another example of Robert Clifford's beautifying of his castle – was intended to impress visitors. In its very early days this would have been the castle's hall, where the garrison ate and slept, while the lord and his family lived on the floor above. The little room between the first and second floors could perhaps have been a guardroom, though it could also have been a treasury.

Carry on up the stairs to the second floor.

The Second Floor
From the second floor, a passage was knocked through at a later date to the top floor of the inner gatehouse, and this later became the lord's chamber. Lady Anne Clifford slept there during her visits to Brougham, and it was in this room that she eventually died.

Before you continue to the top storey, look into the annexe off the stairs at second-floor level.

Cutaway drawing of the keep by Peter Dunn, showing the building as it was used in the late fourteenth century

Right: A decorative corbel on the outside of the keep

Above: Part of the Roman tombstone set in the roof of one of the wall passages in the keep. The inscription translates as: 'To the spirits of the departed. Titus M...lived 32 years more or less. M...his brother set up this inscription.'

Below: The boss, carved with two human heads, at the centre of the vault in the oratory on the top floor of the keep. Skilled carving from around 1300

If you look up at the ceiling, you will see an inscribed Roman tombstone which has been built into the wall – evidence for the re-use of Roman masonry in the construction of the castle. It has been argued that the wording of the inscription shows that there were Christians at Brougham in the years around 300, but this is now disputed.

Carry on up the stairs to the third floor.

The Third Floor

Unlike the floors below, there was a passage around the third-floor chamber, making it slightly smaller than those below, and octagonal as a result of its corners having been cut off.

Walk all the way round the wall passage until you reach the oratory.

From here, you can see the third-floor fireplace, with a fine joggled arch over it, in the north-west corner. The oratory is one of the most remarkable features of the whole castle. Like the whole third floor, the oratory was built by Robert Clifford in around 1300, for his and his family's private devotions. In spite of the fact that it is now quite weathered, it is still possible to appreciate the skill

needed to create the seven-ribbed vault, with its central boss carved in the shape of two heads. Notice also the remains of the figures of a man and a woman carved on the left side of the window. They are probably saints, but they could perhaps represent Edward I and his second wife, Queen Margaret. On the other side of the window is a *piscina* (basin), and facing these, next to a well-made aumbry (cupboard), is a door into a small vestry, where the priest could robe and keep the sacred vessels. To the left of the door, a number of names are carved, with dates from between 1861 and 1918. Some are probably those of local farm-workers who climbed up to the top of the then rickety keep for a dare. Others, elegantly cut in what appears to be identical lettering, may record visits by tourists or antiquaries. The spiral staircase originally continued up for one more flight, onto battlements made all the more impressive by tall turrets at the corners. These have long since disappeared, and the parapet between them is no longer accessible.

Before you make your way down to ground level, look out over the outline of the Roman fort on the south side of the castle.

BROUGHAM CASTLE: TOUR ❖ 19

Lady Anne Clifford had a walled garden laid out across the end of the fort nearest to the castle, extending to the road (its outline is still visible). It was planted with fruit and vegetables, not flowers, producing such delicacies as peas, cucumbers, raspberries and strawberries for Lady Anne and her household.

Once you have finished your visit to the keep, go back downstairs and walk round the outside of the walls.

This will give you a better idea of the castle's position in relation to the Roman fort and the River Eamont.

In medieval times, it was surrounded by moats; they do not appear to have originally contained water, though no doubt they often did so in wet weather. If you go down the steps by the river, round the north side of the inner gatehouse, you will pass the postern which you saw from inside. It opens onto a stair, which in turn leads to a room on the floor above. It was from here that the portcullis was operated, in order to block the passage through into the main courtyard; the slot in which it rose and fell is at the east end of the room. The chamber was lit principally from the north wall by a

The third floor of the keep in the fourteenth century, looking towards the oratory. Reconstruction drawing by Peter Dunn

Aerial view of Brougham as it would have looked in the time of Lady Anne Clifford, complete with a walled garden which would have provided fruit and vegetables for the household. Reconstruction drawing by Peter Dunn

large window, typical of the beginning of the fourteenth century. In the north-west corner are the remains of a fireplace, of the same date. Almost opposite it, in the south wall, is the entrance to a passage which once gave access to the first floor of the keep, and which still leads round to a latrine, with a wash-bowl next to it, almost over the postern gate. Both in this passage and elsewhere on this floor, narrow red stone blocks were used in the facing of the walls; they were inserted as part of the restoration of the castle carried out by the earl of Thanet in the late 1840s, and were left undisturbed when nearly all the rest were removed by the Office of Works as inauthentic in the late 1920s. The refacing of a stretch of the outside of the north wall provides another example of nineteenth-century restoration work.

❖ LADY ANNE CLIFFORD ❖

Lady Anne Clifford was a legend in her own lifetime, and she has remained so ever since. She was one of the greatest figures in the history of north-west England. She was married first to Richard Sackville, earl of Dorset, and later to Philip Herbert, earl of Pembroke, so she was twice a countess by marriage. But later generations have always referred to her as a Clifford, the name she was born with, rather than by one of her married titles, and this has given emphasis to her position as the last in the direct line of a great family whose lordship in Westmorland stretched back into the thirteenth century.

She was herself intensely aware of her dynastic standing. She had the history of her ancestors researched in depth and detail, and the findings were collected into three great 'books of record', which to this day constitute an essential source for the history of the Cliffords. She also gave visual expression to her pride in her ancestry on her own tomb in St Lawrence's Church in Appleby, designed while she was still alive. It bears no image, just twenty-four shields, which set out her lineage in an impressive display of heraldry.

Lady Anne's castles also reflect her identification with her Clifford forbears. Conscious of the antiquity of these great buildings, she was at pains to restore them in a style in keeping with what was there already. As a result, it is not always easy to tell exactly what changes she made. Her self-restraint is all the more striking in the light of her early life, before she retired to Westmorland. She was born in 1590, and as a little girl she was said to have been 'much beloved' by Queen Elizabeth. Her two husbands were both courtiers, as her father had been, and she grew up and spent her early adulthood in and around the court. Since she was intelligent and well-informed, one might have expected her taste to have been influenced by the work of the painters Rubens and Van Dyck, and the architect Inigo Jones, but it was not. As soon as she was able to settle in the North she turned her back on new-fangled metropolitan fashions, preferring those of earlier generations.

In this respect she showed the independence of mind which was typical of her character – a character which was also shaped by many years

Left: Lady Anne Clifford, represented as an elderly woman on a portrait medallion

Below: Lady Anne Clifford's tomb in St Lawrence's Church, Appleby; a magnificent display of heraldry expresses her pride in her family's long and distinguished past

Portrait of Margaret, Countess of Cumberland, Lady Anne Clifford's mother (detail)

of frustration and disappointment. As the only surviving child of the third earl, Lady Anne might have expected to succeed him in the family estates when he died in 1605. But Earl George bequeathed them to his brother Francis and to Francis's heirs, and all Anne's efforts to have the will set aside came to nothing. In spite of the support of her mother, Countess Margaret, to whom she was devoted (her death at Brougham in 1616 was a heavy blow), Lady Anne was not able to secure her family's lands and castles. It was Francis, not Anne, who received James I at Brougham in 1617. To add to her sorrows, neither of her marriages seems to have brought her lasting happiness. Only the possibility that Francis's son Henry would have no heir, in which case the Clifford

❖ THE COUNTESS'S ❖ PILLAR

The Countess's Pillar stands about a quarter of a mile east of Brougham Castle, on the south side of the A66 road to Appleby. About 14ft high, it has sundials on three of its faces, set into one of which is an inscription recording its erection by Lady Anne Clifford to commemorate her last parting there from her dearly-loved mother, Countess Margaret, on 2 April 1616. On the fourth side are the arms of Clifford and Russell, and the date, 1654, of the erection of the pillar. Lady Anne also endowed a charity, making provision for the distribution of £4 on 2 April every year to the poor of the parish, the money being set out on the low stone table next to the pillar. The bishop of Carlisle referred to the pillar in his sermon at Lady Anne's funeral, describing this example of her almsgiving as a 'precious ointment to perfume her pious Mother's memory'. Because it was connected to an endowed charity, the pillar was looked after when the castle was allowed to crumble. It was repaired and gilded in 1758, and again in 1826, while in 1842 it was railed in, the railings being repaired in 1904.

inheritance would revert to her, gave Anne hopes of what she regarded as her rightful inheritance.

Her hopes were fulfilled when Henry died in 1643, but thanks to the Civil Wars it was only six years later, by which time she was nearly sixty, that she was able to travel north, where she remained for the last twenty-seven years of her life. During the 1650s her energies were largely devoted to restoring her estates and castles. She was a staunch Royalist, but when it was suggested to Oliver Cromwell that he should stop her building, he is said to have replied, 'Let her build what she will, she shall not be hindered by me.' Since she had no soldiers, Brougham, Brough and the other castles would in fact have been useless as fortresses. No doubt Cromwell understood this, and appreciated that what she was really doing was converting castles into country mansions, on a scale appropriate to her dignity. Indeed, she moved in stately succession from one castle to another, making each in turn the base from which she exercised her influence and authority, as befitted the last bearer of the Clifford name. The tenants whose rents she raised to pay for the alterations might not have regarded her with reverential eyes. To everyone else she was an almost majestic figure, raised by ancestry,

Lady Anne Clifford arriving at Brougham on 14 October 1670. Reconstruction drawing by Peter Dunn

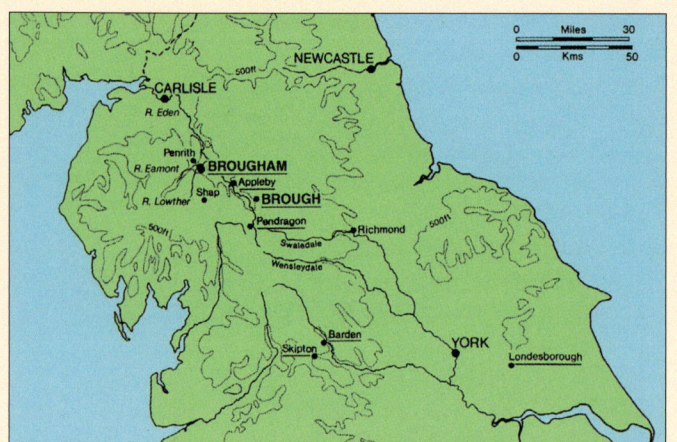

Map of Westmorland, showing the Clifford castles. All were restored by Lady Anne, and she occupied each of them, usually for months at a time, at regular intervals

Right: A fifteenth-century gold ring-brooch found in Whinfell Forest, near Brougham. It is inscribed on the front and back, 'To thee Jesu my trought I plight; and to thee Mary his mother bright.'

wealth and office (she was hereditary sheriff of Westmorland) to a uniquely exalted position in regional society.

Lady Anne owned four castles in Westmorland – Appleby, Brougham, Brough and Pendragon. Appleby, set in the county town, was probably her chief seat, but she occupied them all, moving round them at intervals. On 14 October 1670, for instance, she came into residence at Brougham, and stayed there until 17 August the following year, when she left for Appleby. She remained at Appleby until 17 November, when she moved to Pendragon, staying there until 19 April 1672, when she left for Brough. She stayed there until 15 August, when she departed for Appleby again. From reading Lady Anne's accounts, we know that most of her household went with her, as did huge quantities of 'household stuff' – clothes, hangings and furnishings of all kinds. Forty-four carts and two wagons were needed to transport it all from Brougham to Appleby in June 1668. Members of the local gentry attended Lady Anne as she went, and her arrival in Appleby might have been greeted by the strains of the town musicians and the ringing of church bells.

Lady Anne had her eccentricities, which doubtless grew upon her with age. For instance, she used to distribute not just portraits and medallions of herself, but also large door-locks with her initials carved on them. She would also hang pieces of paper in her bedchamber on which were written sayings and phrases which had caught her attention. Her clothes were unusual enough to be mentioned in the sermon preached at her funeral, being diplomatically described as 'not disliked by any, but imitated by none'. She might also have been a hard landlord, but all the same, there were many who were grateful for her continual presence in the North-west. A devout Christian, she restored churches as well as castles, and was generous in giving alms to travelling musicians and players, as well as to the poor and crippled at her gates. As far as possible, she patronised local craftsmen and shopkeepers, and paid them in cash for their services and goods. Generous to her servants (as long as they behaved themselves), she occasionally contributed to the marriage portions of her laundrymaids, and once helped one of her officers to buy himself an estate. Not surprisingly, many of her employees stayed in her service for years.

Lady Anne had been devoted to her mother, and she was herself an affectionate mother, grandmother and eventually great-grandmother. Her diaries record the pleasure she took in visits from members of her family, especially if she could send them off to inspect and admire one of her castles. After the battering these had received over the years, either through neglect or from involvement in the Civil Wars, she was entitled to be proud of the care she had lavished on bringing them back to life. Indeed, it might have cost her as much as £40,000. She set up inscriptions to mark her restorations, each one concluding with a reference to a passage in Isaiah, chosen to show how she saw herself:

And they that shall be of thee shall build the old waste places: thou shalt raise up the foundations of many generations; and thou shalt be called, the repairer of the breach, the restorer of paths to dwell in.

Clifford triptych commissioned by Lady Anne, who is shown in her late fifties in the right-hand panel. She is austerely, but not yet eccentrically, dressed

26 ❖ Brougham Castle

BROUGH CASTLE ❖ 27

BROUGH CASTLE

The Brewhouse, Bakehouse and Kitchen
These were built by Lady Anne Clifford in the seventeenth century

Clifford's Tower
Lady Anne's chamber stood on the top floor

The Keep
This was the heart of the castle. The basement was used as a store, with chambers above

The Stables
Horses were vital into the seventeenth century for transporting men and goods

The Gatehouse
This was originally three storeys high. The top floor was used as a guest chamber

The Hall Range
The hall was on the first floor, with storerooms and guest rooms below. On the top floor was the Great Chamber, where senior members of the household usually ate

Roman Fort
The castle was built on the remains of a Roman fort

PETER DUNN

BROUGH CASTLE
HISTORY

The Castle on the Ridge

The oldest parts of Brough Castle date from around 1100, when what is now north-west England had only just been annexed by William Rufus from the kingdom of the Scots. It was originally built to safeguard the routes from the North, both across the Pennines into Yorkshire and more directly south into Westmorland and Lancashire. Excavations in the 1920s showed that it was from the first built at least partly of stone, and that the present keep rests on the Norman masonry of an earlier tower; similar stonework survives in stretches of the curtain wall. The layout of the castle as seen today, with the keep standing at one end of a bailey or courtyard, is probably the same as its late eleventh-century predecessor. These powerful defences were dictated by pressing military needs. The loss of the old counties of Cumberland and Westmorland was resented by successive Scottish kings, who made repeated attempts to recover them, finally admitting defeat only in 1237.

It was one of these attempts at reconquest that provides us with our first clear glimpse of Brough Castle. In 1173, and again in 1174,

Aerial view of Brough Castle

King William the Lion invaded the north of England. In 1174 he left Carlisle blockaded, and marched south with his main army. Appleby quickly surrendered, then Brough was attacked. The contemporary writer Jordan Fantosme tells in his verse-chronicle how the castle was defended by six knights — in other words by a substantial garrison, for they would have been important men, each with a retinue. Even so the bailey was soon captured, and the defenders retreated to the keep. He describes how the attackers then set fire to the keep, which suggests that it had a stone base and a wooden superstructure. This is borne out by Fantosme's account of what happened next. One of the knights, newly dubbed and probably anxious to display his courage and

❖ THE REY CROSS ❖ ON STAINMORE

The Rey Cross, which stands beside the road about six miles east of Brough, traditionally marked the ancient border between England and Scotland, before it was pushed back to the Solway Firth in 1092. (The word 'Rey' is probably of Norse origin, meaning boundary.) As late as 1258 the bishop of Glasgow still claimed that it marked the southern limit of his diocese. It has long lost its original shape, but it has been suggested that there was once a wheel-head cross set on its shaft, which according to seventeenth-century antiquarians (of uncertain reliability) was carved on one side with 'the picture and armes of the king of England, and on the other the image of the king and kingdome of Scotland'. Each monarch was represented as looking back upon his own territory. Its position on the lonely and exposed road over the Pennines made it an appropriate place for a hospice for pilgrims and travellers. The hospice was founded some time before 1171, when it was given to the nuns of Marrick, a few miles west of Richmond. They paid its chaplain £4 a year until their house was dissolved in 1540.

The Rey Cross on Stainmore

The keep of Brough Castle, seen from inside the courtyard; powerful defensive work of the late twelfth century

The south curtain wall of Brough Castle, with Clifford's Tower (built by Robert Clifford at the end of the thirteenth century) at the near end

warlike skills, refused to surrender when his fellows did so. Not only did he hurl down spears with deadly results, but he followed these with pointed stakes, presumably pulled out of a palisade, before he finally gave up the struggle. The siege ended with the destruction of 'almost all' of the keep; what survived would have been the lower levels, made of masonry.

These remains provided the base for a new keep, which is the one seen today, built in the late twelfth century. It provided the focal point of the castle. In 1203 King John gave Brough, along with Appleby and the lordship of Westmorland, to Robert de Vieuxpont, the builder of Brougham. Vieuxpont built at Brough, too; the gatehouse is largely his work, and he probably also constructed a hall across the south end of the courtyard. But his immediate descendants neglected the castle, and in 1254 it was reported to be run-down, the keep being succinctly described as 'decayed'. The fact that the hall was later replaced may indicate that it was allowed to collapse.

Brough under the Cliffords

Brough, like Brougham, passed to the Cliffords in 1268. Robert Clifford carried out important works here, just as he did at Brougham. He built a new hall, on the same site as Vieuxpont's, though narrower, and at its south end he built the semicircular tower, now known as 'Clifford's Tower', as a residence for himself and his family. He also undertook a substantial restoration of the curtain walls — a necessary measure in view of the threat posed by Scottish raiders from across the border. The village of Brough was devastated in 1314 and again in 1319. No doubt the castle gave shelter to the villagers, with their livestock and goods. It also accommodated a large garrison, and fifteen men-at-arms and twenty 'hobelers' (heavy and light cavalry respectively) were reported there in the early 1320s. The demand for lodging and stabling must have been considerable.

Further works were carried out at Brough in the late fourteenth century, in the time of Roger Clifford, as at Brougham. These had an important impact on the castle's layout. The earlier hall was replaced, again as at Brougham, by a first-floor hall set over a basement. This new hall was placed against the south curtain wall, between Clifford's Tower and the gatehouse. Brough escaped capture in the great Scottish invasion of 1388 in which Brougham and Appleby were sacked. Indeed, when members of the Clifford family came to Westmorland in the years immediately afterwards, they usually stayed at Brough. Perhaps this explains why they added to Roger's hall, constructing a range of domestic buildings along its north side, as well as refacing the front of the gatehouse. This was probably the work of Roger's grandson Thomas, who was killed at the first battle of St Alban's in 1455, fighting for Henry VI.

When the Cliffords re-established themselves in Westmorland after the Battle of Bosworth Field in 1485, they continued to stay at Brough. Clearly they made more than passing visits, for it was after Henry Clifford had celebrated 'a great Christmas' there in 1521 that a fire devastated the whole castle. It seems to have burnt out all its wooden fittings – floors, doors, windows and the like – and left it uninhabitable, not to be occupied again until Lady Anne Clifford took it in hand, as she did all her other castles.

Brough's Renaissance

The structure of the castle must have been basically sound, for work began in 1659, and in the following year was sufficiently advanced for Lady Anne to be able to make a brief visit, staying one night in Clifford's Tower and two in the keep. An inscription recording her restoration was put up at the end of 1663, so the work was probably finished by then. But although she spent eight days in the castle in the following year, she made no lengthy stay until 1665, when she arrived on 10 November and stayed until 19 April the following year. She was to make extended visits on a further three occasions, always occupying the chamber at the top of Clifford's Tower.

Henry Clifford, 5th Earl of Cumberland (1590–1643) and first cousin of Lady Anne Clifford. She inherited Brough and Brougham from him in 1643, later making Brough inhabitable for the first time since 1521, when the castle was devastated by fire while their great-great-grandfather was celebrating 'a great Christmas' there

Lady Anne made some substantial additions to the fabric of Brough. As well as restoring the existing buildings, she built the block of stables between the gatehouse and the keep, and also the row of service buildings at the east end of the north curtain wall.

Later History

After Lady Anne's death, Brough, like Brougham, was neglected, though minor repairs to keep the roofs sound went on being made until 1714. But in the following year most of the roofs and fittings were sold, for a total of £155. There were significant exceptions from the sale: the stables, along with parts of the gatehouse and hall, were reserved by Lord Thanet so that they could be converted into a courtroom complex for the manor of Brough. How long they were used for this purpose is not recorded, but perhaps not for very long. An engraving of 1739 shows that by then the stables had disappeared, and it was later reported that in 1763 a good deal of Clifford's Tower was demolished to provide stone for Brough Mill. Thereafter little effort seems to have been made to preserve the fabric of the buildings. A report in 1919 recorded extensive robbing of the stonework in the past – 'moulded stones, lintels, staircase treads and pavements have been taken away' – and in the following year, on 20 May 1920, not long after the castle had been placed in the guardianship of the Ministry of Works, the south-west corner of the keep fell down. The consolidation of the buildings which followed probably came only just in time.

Engraving of Brough Castle in 1739, by the Buck Brothers. The roofs and window glass have gone, and the stables have disappeared, but most of the walls still stand to their full height

BROUGH CASTLE TOUR

The plan of the castle on the inside back cover should help you to find your way round.

As you make your way towards the gatehouse, look around at the castle's setting.

Lying at the northern end of the earthworks surrounding the Roman camp of *Verteris*, Brough Castle stands in a position of natural strength on a steep slope, further protected by the Swindall Beck which runs below its north face. This was the side on which the castle was most likely to be attacked. Consequently, the domestic buildings line the south curtain wall, and it is their windows which overlook the approach to the gatehouse.

THE GATEHOUSE

Sadly shrunken today, the gatehouse was originally three storeys high. In the seventeenth century, and probably earlier, the top floor was used as a guest chamber. The first and second floors each had a three-light window on this outer side of the gatehouse, while between the first floor and the gateway arch a stone slab (now sadly lost) once recorded Lady Anne Clifford's restoration of the castle (it was removed in the

The battered remains of the gatehouse, originally the work of Robert de Vieuxpont shortly after 1200

The remains of the stables

The exterior of the keep

eighteenth century for the sake of the lead and iron holding it in place, and later put under the water-wheel of Brough mill!) On either side of the entrance there was formerly a pyramid-shaped buttress; these seem to have been ornamental, although the gatehouse was designed to resist attack. Even in Lady Anne's time there was a nail-studded gate opening into the arch. In earlier times there was probably a portcullis and also a drawbridge.

Walk through the gatehouse arch and stop when you reach the information panel just inside the courtyard.

The Courtyard

As you go through the arch, notice the stairs on the right which led up to the hall and the other chambers set against the south curtain wall. The basic layout of the castle is probably much the same as it has always been – a long and narrow, stone walled enclosure, with the keep (the heart of the defences) at one end, and the domestic buildings at the other, first against the east wall and later in the south-east corner.

Turn left and walk towards the keep.

The Stables

The first building you come to was once the stables, occupying most of the space between the gatehouse and the keep. It probably had garners for hay and oats at first-floor level. The size of the stables acts as a reminder that in the seventeenth century (and later), horses remained vital for transporting both men and goods. Lady Anne herself travelled between her castles in a coach drawn by six horses, until in old age she preferred to be carried in a horse litter. In earlier centuries, of course, men had also ridden out to war on horseback.

Carry on round the courtyard to the keep.

The Keep

The keep was never intended to be beautiful, although when its four corner-turrets were intact it must certainly have been imposing. Though plain, there are some decorative elements. The exterior is divided horizontally by two continuous off-sets, which go right round it. On the north and south sides the upper string courses support what appear

to be ornamental pilasters. It has been suggested that the curious rows of little openings just below the parapet on the east and south sides were intended to provide nesting places for pigeons, but it seems more likely that they, too, were meant to be purely decorative.

As at Brougham, the entrance was not originally on the ground floor, as it is now, but on the first floor. In Lady Anne's time there was a flight of stone stairs running parallel to the east wall, which led to a round-headed door, probably just a few feet above the ground. The base of these stairs can still be seen, but the doorway has vanished, along with most of the east wall. In the middle ages, the doorway was reached through a forebuilding, which was an extra obstacle for attackers who broke into the castle bailey, like the Scots in 1174.

Walk round to the right of the keep and through the door into the basement.

The basement served as a store for the upper floors, and it was originally entered by stairs from the floor above. The door in the north wall was made by Lady Anne. The plaster, the remains of which can still be seen on the walls, was applied not only to improve the basement's hygiene, but also to make it appear lighter. In this way, light was reflected from the window (which was probably divided in the seventeenth century, to admit light on either side of a partition) or from lamps and candles.

There is no way up to the upper floors of the keep now. Originally the keep had only two storeys over the basement, connected by a spiral staircase in the north-east corner, with a steeply gabled roof above them (you can see its outline against the inside of the walls). This was later replaced by a higher roof, which allowed room for an additional floor. In Lady Anne's time this top floor was partitioned to make two guest chambers, each with two beds. The new roof was highly unusual. Neither flat nor pointed, it was said by the late-seventeenth-century antiquary Thomas Machell (who also provided a rather clumsy drawing of it) to have been designed in a 'quite contrarie way', so that rainwater did not pour off through gutters, but instead collected in an indentation in the middle. The reason for this apparently eccentric

Above: The interior of the keep, showing the different floor levels

Above left: The remains of the forebuilding and the original entrance to the keep

Thomas Machell's sketch of the roof of the keep, showing how it was designed to catch rainwater

arrangement lay in the feature which is most obviously missing from the castle plan, namely a well. No trace of one has ever been found in the castle. Machell's plan contains a well, but it is outside the gatehouse. The unusual shape of the roof represents an ingenious attempt to give the garrison a water supply to fall back on in time of siege.

Leave the keep and carry on walking round the courtyard.

(The rough sandstone paving in the courtyard is probably essentially medieval). Just a little way along the north curtain wall is a well-preserved double latrine set into the wall, discharging into the Swindale Beck below.

Carry on round the courtyard.

THE BREWHOUSE, BAKEHOUSE AND KITCHEN

In the north-east corner of the courtyard can be seen the remains of three small buildings – a brewhouse, a bakehouse and a kitchen. All were built by Lady Anne Clifford, as part of her refurbishment of the castle. A fourth building, a coalhole (no longer visible), was put up in 1669 (at that time the castle paid hearth tax on twenty-four chimneys). The coalhole was a roofless enclosure, but the other buildings were depicted in the seventeenth century as one storey high, with a continuous slate roof. Each was entered through a round-headed door, and there were five windows for the three rooms. Doors and windows have now vanished, but in the kitchen there are still traces of two fireplaces facing one another in the east and west walls; the latter is set deep into the wall, and must also have served as an oven. By the later middle ages the kitchen was on the opposite side of the castle to the hall

Thomas Machell's sketch of the castle and late seventeenth-century plan, showing how Brough Castle was used in the time of Lady Anne Clifford

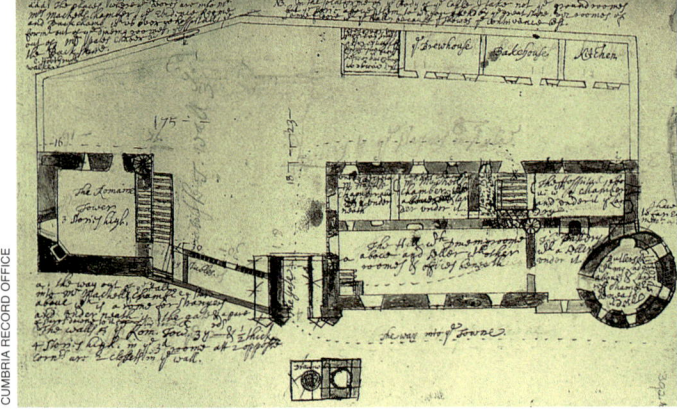

(the original hall, set against the east curtain wall, would have been relatively close to the kitchen).

THE HALL RANGE

From the late fourteenth century, food had to be carried over the courtyard to the buildings whose ruins you can see in the south-east corner of the castle. It is important to remember that what you see here are mostly the walls of ground-floor chambers, nearly all of them basements and store-rooms. The life of the castle went on mostly in the upper rooms, which have largely disappeared, except for their windows in the outer walls.

Cross the courtyard and walk through the room on the left to the far south-east corner of the castle.

The Laundress's Room

The ground floor of this semicircular tower, known as Clifford's Tower, was the laundress's room in the late seventeenth century. Its rectangular windows, with their solid lintels and frames, are part of Lady Anne Clifford's restoration. It is probably no accident that they are reminiscent of Tudor workmanship. The castle had been made uninhabitable by fire in 1521, and with her usual care for period detail Lady Anne brought it back to life to look as she believed it would have done had that disaster never happened.

The Hall

The rest of the buildings in this corner of the courtyard are at first sight a mass of shapeless and roofless structures, all the harder to understand for being made up of the ruins of two parallel ranges, one against the south curtain wall, built in the late fourteenth century, the other, set alongside the first, built in the mid-fifteenth century. If you look up towards the outer wall, you will see in it the remains of two medieval windows, which once lit the hall. Like the hall at Brougham, this room was on the first floor, and was heated either by a fireplace set into a side wall or by a central hearth. Below the hall was a cellar, along with what the late-seventeenth-century plan calls 'other roomes & offices beneath'. These would have been primarily storerooms, but it is possible that they were used for accommodation when space ran short, perhaps for servants and grooms.

A stretch of the north curtain wall

Clifford's Tower from the outside, showing the heavy Tudor-style rectangular windows inserted by Lady Anne

The remains of the two ranges of buildings set against the south curtain wall, in the south-east corner of the courtyard

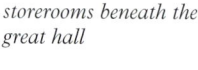

One of three vaulted storerooms beneath the great hall

Walk out into the courtyard again, turn left and go into the next room along. Go through to the inner room.

At the far end is the remains of a latrine. This suggests that this room might also have been used as living quarters.

Although there were stairs up from the gatehouse, the rooms in the upper storeys of the two ranges, including the hall, would usually have been reached from the courtyard, by a stairway built by Lady Anne. If you return to the outer room you will see its remains, still visible at ground level. (In the seventeenth century, the two, central, inner-range rooms were used as a laundry and a larder respectively.)

The Great Chamber

From the hall a spiral staircase led up to the great chamber on the top floor. This room served as a dining-room, where the senior members of the household usually ate. When Lady Anne came to stay at Brough, she would have walked through this room, and then through another room at its east end, before reaching her own chamber at the top of Clifford's Tower. Other rooms on the top two floors included chambers for her steward and secretary, and for the butler (his room was also in Clifford's Tower, on the floor below Lady Anne's). There was also a room for the cook, and at least two guestrooms. In addition, there was a little 'evidence room', where papers and valuables were kept, at the top of the stairs on the first floor.

THE CHURCH OF ST MICHAEL

It is interesting that there is no record of a chapel at Brough. The church of St Michael stands close to the castle, and much of its nave is of the same age as the earlier parts of the castle, most obviously the south door's round-headed doorway. When Gabriel Vincent, Lady Anne's steward, died in the keep in 1666, his body was taken to the church for burial. He lies now under a tomb slab on the floor of the nave near the pulpit which describes him, in words surely chosen by his employer, as 'chief director of all her buildings in the north'. The occupants of the castle, whether they were soldiers or civilians, probably worshipped in this church. Perhaps its parson sometimes led prayers in the castle at Brough, as the vicar certainly did at Brougham when Lady Anne was in residence.

Lady Anne Clifford has long been considered the presiding genius of these two castles, because of her building works and her long and remarkable life. Brough, however, had a resident spirit of a rather humbler kind as well, in the form of a genial pixie called Hobthrush, who was said to inhabit a hole in the north curtain wall, quite possibly the double latrine which can still be seen not far from the keep. Among his other acts of kindness, he might be persuaded to work overnight at harvest-time, bringing the stacked corn into the barns of those who put out a gift for him.

View of the fells and the Pennines from the top of the keep

Bibliography

D.J.H. Clifford ed., *The Diaries of Lady Anne Clifford*, 1990

W.D. Simpson, 'Brough under Stainmore: the castle and the church', *Transactions of the Cumberland Westmorland Antiquarian and Archaeological Society*, second series 46 (1946), pp. 223-83

R.T. Spence, *Lady Anne Clifford*, 1997

H. Summerson, S. Harrison and M. Trueman, *Brougham Castle, Cumbria*, Cumberland and Westmorland Antiquarian and Archaeological Society, Research Series 8, 1998

Royal Commission on the Historical Monuments of England: Westmorland, 1936

The antiquarian Thomas Machell's account of Brough Castle survives in the Cumbria Record Office, Carlisle, in *Manuscripts of the Dean and Chapter of Carlisle*, MS Machell 1, pp. 392–6

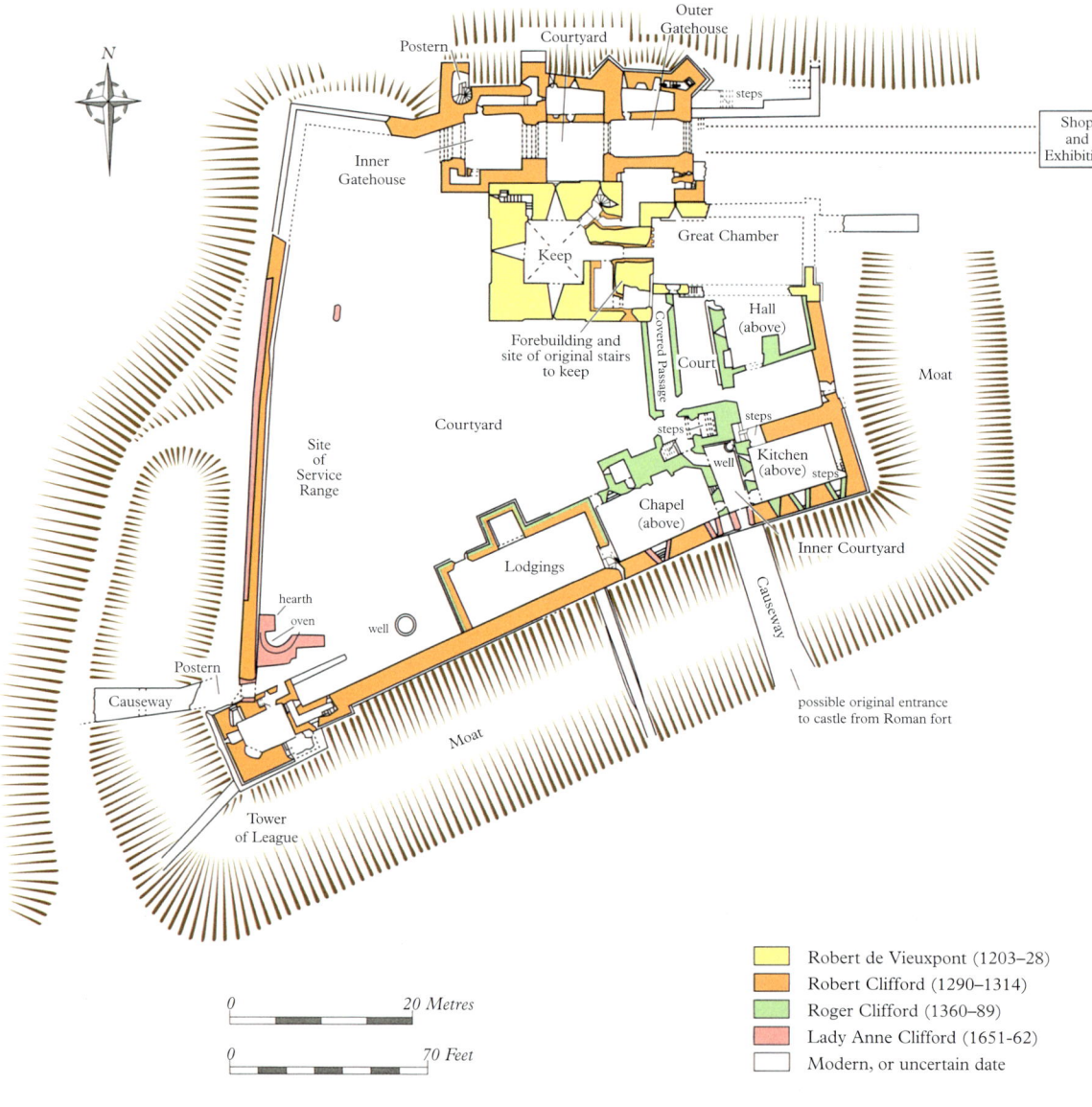